BUILDING JOB SKILLS™

DEVELOP YOUR
INTERPERSONAL
SKILLS
AT WORK

Elissa Thompson and Michael A. Sommers

Rosen
YA™

New York

Published in 2020 by The Rosen Publishing Group, Inc.
29 East 21st Street, New York, NY 10010

First Edition

Library of Congress Cataloging-in-Publication Data

Names: Thompson, Elissa, author. | Sommers, Michael A., 1966– author.
Title: Develop your interpersonal skills at work / Elissa Thompson and Michael A. Sommers.
Description: First edition. | New York : Rosen Publishing, 2020. | Series: Building job skills |
Includes bibliographical references and index.
Identifiers: LCCN 2019013992 | ISBN 9781725347137 (library bound) |
ISBN 9781725347120 (pbk.)
Subjects: LCSH: Business communication—Juvenile literature. | Interpersonal relations—
Juvenile literature. | Interpersonal communication—Juvenile literature.
Classification: LCC HF5718 .T46353 2020 | DDC 650.1/3—dc23
LC record available at https://lccn.loc.gov/2019013992

Manufactured in the United States of America

CONTENTS

INTRODUCTION

Go team go!

You've been hearing about the importance of teamwork since preschool. You've been assigned group projects at school. You've spent tons of time with your friends. Maybe you've even played a sport, working together to win against another team. And if you have a job, you know what it's like to work with and for other people: coworkers, bosses, and customers, too. You could be a coffee shop barista, serving caffeine up quickly to tired and cranky customers. You could be an intern at a local politician's office, handling locals with lots of opinions. No matter your job, at work you must learn to handle all different types of new relationships.

Your first few jobs are a great chance to see what you might want to do with your life. First jobs are also a great opportunity to meet people different from yourself. You can gain new perspectives about the world. A job can also help you learn how to deal with all sorts of people who you may never have encountered before. Because, remember, your boss is not your parent or your friend. Your customers are just that, people paying for a service that you are providing. All of this may be new territory to you, but by mastering some interpersonal skills, you'll be ready to wow everyone.

Being successful at work means learning to relate to all sorts of different people: coworkers, customers, bosses, and more.

Having a job as a teen can be great for your confidence, your future career, and your schooling.

Research shows that teens who have jobs get more than just a paycheck. According to an article in *Harvard Business Review*, you can increase your desire to go to a two- or four-year college. You can craft a better résumé and succeed at future job interviews. You're also more likely to reduce your school absences for the following year. And the more school you attend, the better your grades will probably be.

Being able to work well with people is an important skill that will help you throughout your entire life. You will need to work with coworkers as your career grows, no matter in what direction. Being known as a team player can help you to move ahead to better positions and more exciting opportunities. By being easy to work with and helpful to others, people will want to see you succeed. They may even help you along the way.

Of course, teamwork isn't always easy. Conflict can arise in any situation. You are already aware that people fight, like you do with your siblings, your friends, or even your parents. But fighting at work can be different. You have to handle the problem thoughtfully. It might not be your fault. But how you deal with conflict is very important. By being assertive and making sure you are heard—while still considering other viewpoints—you can learn to stand up for yourself.

By learning how to relate to your coworkers, bosses, and customers, you will be ready to take on the world!

CHAPTER ONE

COMMUNICATING AT WORK

C ommunicating with friends is very different from talking to someone at work. If you want to tell your best friend something, you might send a quick text full of emojis. While you are on the job, you need to think about with whom you're communicating. If you are talking with your boss, you should be thoughtful when speaking. To get your point across in an effective and positive way, you need to think about what you want to say, why you want to say it, and how you're going to communicate your message. Whether you're providing instruction, asking a question, or firing off a quick email, the message that you send is not always the message that the person on the other end receives.

SPOKEN AND NONSPOKEN MESSAGING

While at work, you want your message to be clear and unambiguous. What another person understands or concludes from your words can vary greatly from your intended point. And you want to be understood,

Communicating at work is a lot different from chatting with friends or fighting with siblings. Be thoughtful and choose your moment before speaking up.

right? When you speak, you are communicating with so much more than just words. You also send messages via your body language, your tone, and even how far away you're standing from the other person. Albert Mehrabian, a famous verbal and nonverbal communication researcher, found in the

1960s and 1970s that about 7 percent of your message are the words you actually use. Fifty-five percent is nonverbal, and 38 percent is vocal, including your tone and inflection.

So how can you control your nonverbal messaging? Here are some strategies to consider, from the American Association for the Advancement of Science:

- **Eye contact:** Look in the eyes of the person you are speaking to. Don't stare at the ground or at your phone. Eye contact helps increase your credibility.
- **Posture:** Stand up straight, shoulders back. If seated, don't slouch. This will help with eye contact, too. Try not to fidget with your hands. If you need to, hold a pen and a piece of paper, like you are going to take notes.
- **Tone:** Try to put inflection into your voice. Add feelings to your words instead of speaking in a monotone. Also avoid your voice range going up at the end of every sentence. You don't want to sound like you are asking a question when you are really making a statement.

Jeanie needed to ask her boss a question about a customer's order. She shuffled her feet into his office and stared out the window while mumbling at him. All of these factors had a big effect on her boss's perception of Jeanie. She seemed not very interested in her work, or invested in what was going on. She sounded as if she didn't know what she was talking about. She was perceived by how she was communicating. Imagine if Jeanie had entered her boss's office after a confident

CONTEXT, CLUSTERS, AND CONGRUENCE

Many social scientists say that it's not just about the 55/38/7 ratio that Mehrabian discovered decades ago. As Jeff Thompson, PhD, wrote in *Psychology Today*, it's also about context, clusters, and congruence. By taking all these factors into consideration, you can better control how you communicate and how you understand others.

Context: Context refers to the situation at hand. Some situations might require more formal behavior. This behavior might seem stiff, awkward, or uncomfortable in another setting. Are you at work? Then you should adopt a professional tone, and you should also be addressed this way. If you are hanging out with your friends, you can all be more informal.

Clusters: Consider the situation as a whole. Who is speaking to you? Are they yelling or whispering? Are they leaning into you or sitting far away?

Congruence: Think about whether what someone says matches up with what their nonverbal language is telling you. As Thompson writes, "Do the spoken words match the tone and the body language? After someone falls, and they verbally state they are fine, however their face is grimacing and their voice is shaky, you might want to probe a little deeper."

Take the total of all of these variables into consideration while at work. This way, you can better understand what is being said—and what is meant by those words.

knock. She spoke in a calm, firm voice while looking him in the eye, smiling. She had good posture. The same message was much more clearly heard. Jeanie seemed more impressive and authoritative. Her boss was impressed.

If you're communicating via telephone, the person or people you're talking with can't see you. Nonetheless, they will still be able to make judgments about you based on such details as the volume and tone of your voice. These judgments will affect how they perceive you. It will also affect their perception of the message you are trying to get across. If during a phone conversation with your boss, for example, you sound impatient or in a rush, it won't matter what you're saying. Your boss will likely think you're not paying attention or are not interested in the subject under discussion. He or she may grow annoyed. However, what if you spoke to your boss calmly, using an enthusiastic tone and encouraging questions and feedback? Your conversation will be much more successful and agreeable for both of you.

BEFORE YOU HIT SEND

"Just text me!" You've probably said that phrase or heard it many times. According to the *Chicago Tribune*, US smartphone users send five times as many texts as

Written work communication should be professional and error free.
Read emails over at least once before hitting Send.

phone calls each day. They spend 26 minutes texting a day versus six minutes talking on the phone. But texting and email can lead to miscommunication. Think about everything you can learn from nonverbal communication in a conversation. All of that information is missing in an email, stripping your message down. However, there are ways to make sure you communicate effectively via the written word.

In an email, people tend to focus on details. Spelling mistakes can distract from your message. They're the written equivalent of staring out the window while giving an oral report. Other details can also affect your communication. For instance, the way you sign off can have an impact on the entire content of your email. "See ya" might seem too familiar or even rude in a situation where you barely know somebody. A good way to sign off any work email is, "Thank you." Adopt the same professional tone in writing you would use while speaking to your boss or a coworker. If you're unsure if you are getting your message across, or if you are sending a very important email, ask someone else to read it over before you hit Send. If no one is available, print it out and read it aloud. You will catch mistakes you might not see on your screen.

LISTENING UP AND BEING HEARD

Communication is a two-way street. Many people are great talkers. However, the ability to listen well is a valuable skill. Being a good listener is about more than just hearing the words coming out of someone's mouth. It involves giving your full attention and really digesting a speaker's or writer's message. This is something you can't do if you're looking at Instagram on your phone. In a face-to-face meeting, listening means looking directly at the speaker. Make sure you understand the message. If you don't, ask questions. If you can't hear or understand something, politely ask the speaker to talk louder or slower, or to repeat himself or herself. It is your responsibility, just as much as his or hers, to make sure that the communication flows smoothly and that everybody fully understands the points being expressed.

STEP AWAY FROM YOUR PHONE

Distraction can be a roadblock to communication. If you're having trouble listening to others at work, consider turning off your phone. Put it in your bag and don't look at it until it's time to go home. If this feels too difficult, why not let your parents and closest friends know you'll be offline for a few hours. By starting out slowly, you can learn how to distance yourself. You don't need to check your group texts while at work. It can wait. Promise.

EXTERNAL AND INTERNAL DISTRACTIONS

Even when you are paying attention, that doesn't mean that your boss, coworker, or customer is tuned in to your conversation or email. Remember that any single message—particularly one sent and received during a busy workday—can be affected by distractions. Distractions can be external or internal.

External distractions are those caused by the surrounding environment. Examples of such

Putting away your phone at work can help you pay attention to what's happening around you. Social media can wait.

interruptions include disruptive telephone calls, people barging in to talk, and background noise such as passing traffic.

Internal distractions happen inside someone's mind. They include unwanted thoughts, lack of sleep, or stress.

If you sense someone is distracted, you can suggest moving to a calmer environment. Focus on speaking slowly and clearly with lots of eye contact. Ask questions to make sure the person understands everything you're saying. Encourage feedback.

By learning how to communicate effectively at work, you will be on your way to becoming a valued employee.

CHAPTER TWO

MAKING CONNECTIONS

ou have all sorts of relationships in your life: close friends, acquaintances, relatives, teachers, and more. You generally have the freedom to choose with whom you want to hang out, and when. At a job, however, you often have no choice who you're spending time with.

During your life, you are going to spend a lot of time at work. Having good work relationships is an essential part of being happy and productive at your job. But how do you create these good relationships? Figuring out how to get along with coworkers is an important part of any position.

Making new relationships at work can be fulfilling and fun. Your coworkers can help you out, answer questions, and make the day go by quickly.

Navigating differences and working together effectively is where interpersonal skills come in.

RELATING TO OTHERS

On any given day at your job, you may deal with a few people, or you may deal with many: colleagues, managers, bosses, interns, customers, and delivery people. You don't need to like these people, but you do need to work with them. More than that, you need to work well together. This involves more than you just doing your job while they do theirs and expecting that everything else will take care of itself. Often, working well with others depends upon your ability to manage relationships.

Relationships need to develop in order to thrive. If you ignore other people's needs and show no concern for their problems, your relationships with them will likely suffer. In well-managed relationships, people feel motivated. They have a sense of camaraderie. This makes it easier to work toward a common goal.

Here are some easy steps, from *Fast Company* magazine, that you can take to build relationships at work. You don't have to be best friends with your coworkers, but your shift will go by a lot faster if everyone gets along.

- **Have a good attitude:** Sure, everyone complains about work sometimes, but try being positive. Instead of getting involved in work drama, focus on your own responsibilities.

Making friends at work is just like growing relationships in any other part of your life. Be thoughtful and considerate, and you will do great.

- **Offer to help:** You certainly should not do someone else's job, but everyone needs a hand once in a while. If your coworker is rushing to finish stuffing envelopes before the mailman comes by, and you are all done with your own work, offer to pitch in.
- **Say hello:** Greet people when you see them. Remember their names, and ask about their lives. If they got a new pet, ask to see a picture. If they were under the weather last week, ask how they are feeling now. By recalling small pieces of information about

people, you are showing you are thoughtful, a great quality in a coworker.

TROUBLE AND TENSION

Of course, sometimes you'll have to deal with people who have difficult attitudes or personalities. If you're starting a new job, an employee who has been around for a long time might feel threatened by you. He might want to call all the shots or blame you whenever something goes wrong. Or a colleague might

HOW TO DEAL

You're not getting along with your coworker and you've begun dreading going to a job you once loved. Here are some tips from Deepak Chopra, a well-known author and speaker, written for Oprah.com, that may help:

- "When you feel really frustrated, go someplace in private and vent your frustrations. It's okay to scream if nobody overhears you. Bring a pillow, name it after them and and shout it out."
- "At home, take some time every day to close your eyes and find your center. When you get good at it, take the practice to work with you. A few minutes' break is all you need to go inside and stabilize."
- "At least one hour a day, email or call someone whom you really enjoy talking to. Being in constant contact with friends has been proven highly effective by those researching happiness."

unfairly blame you because she was friends with the person who had the job before and was fired. For this reason, she might resent you or think you're doing everything wrong.

You may try to be polite to such coworkers and to talk to them about any problems they might have. Unfortunately, if these people are very difficult, your attempts might not be successful. Such situations can leave you feeling stressed, confused, and unmotivated to go to work. You may spend a lot of time hoping the offending person will change, get transferred, or even fired so that you can actually look forward to work. However, wishing for change is a waste of time. No matter how much you might wish it, some people may never see your point of view. In the end, the only person you can ever change is yourself.

TAKING CHARGE, NOT CONTROL

Unfortunately, in life, there will be many situations over which you'll have no control. But instead of being miserable, try to accept that there are times when you really *can't* be in control of a situation. However, although you can't be in control, you can be in charge.

When you try to be in control, it means you are trying to get others to accept the way you think things should be. When that doesn't happen, you may feel frustrated or angry because others are keeping you from reaching your goal. In comparison, being in charge means that you accept a situation for what it is—not the way you wish it would be. Once you do this, you can work with and around any difficulties in your path to meet your goals as best you can.

In terms of managing relationships, being in charge means that when people are being difficult, you try to see where they are coming from. Why is it affecting you? Why are they behaving in this manner? What are their goals? Often, conflict develops when people have different goals. Look at your own attitudes. Are you able to see their points of view? Do you sympathize or empathize with their problems?

When you have figured out what's really happening and why, you can try to manage the situation by making changes to the relationship. You can do this by attempting to get rid of or reducing negative aspects while concentrating on the good. Lindy's coworker Julie was extremely bossy. It really bothered Lindy, so much so that Lindy couldn't see how good Julie was with customers. Lindy shifted her focus to how Julie handled difficult or cranky visitors to the store in an easy and friendly manner. She tried to pay attention to and learn from Julie. By focusing on Julie's good qualities instead of her bossiness, Lindy was able to develop a better and more productive relationship with Julie.

Learning to build relationships at work can make you a happy and productive coworker.

MYTHS & FACTS

Myth: Working through lunch at your desk shows you're committed.
Fact: It can be a good idea to take a break at lunch. If you're having a tough time dealing with a coworker, take a moment to recharge. "During your lunch break, do something you really love. Even if the activity lasts only a few minutes, it takes you to a place where irritating people can't intrude," Chopra wrote on Oprah.com.

Myth: Small talk is distracting and should be avoided.
Fact: Chatting with your coworkers is okay! Ask about their favorite sports team, or what they did over the weekend. Be mindful of cues that someone is busy and don't forget about your own work. But stopping to talk for a minute or two is a great way to engage with your coworkers.

Myth: Leave your personal life at home.
Fact: While you are at work you should of course act professionally. Show up on time, do your tasks, help out when needed. But you should also be yourself. You don't need to overshare about your life or that fight you just had with your boyfriend, but you can still be true to yourself and who you are. You were hired for this job for a reason. Let yourself shine!

CHAPTER THREE

THE POWER OF TEAMWORK

You may have done group projects at school, or played a team sport. Maybe you've worked with your siblings or cousins to help out at home. So you probably understand what it's like to be part of a team. When you have a job, you are on a team with your coworkers. By working together, you get things done. For this reason, employers place enormous value on people who work well in teams or groups. It doesn't matter whether your job is in a restaurant or at a major international company. Teamwork is often the most efficient, least expensive, and sometimes only way to get a job done.

Teamwork on the field can be similar to teamwork at your job. Working together can help you solve problems and succeed.

THERE'S NO "I" IN TEAM

When you hear the word "team," you may think of a sports team. On a soccer, volleyball, or basketball team the players are on the same side. Their goal is to beat the opposition. Team members train together and depend upon each other. They make the most of each player's particular skills and talents. When team members work well together, they can meet the goals set by their coach or manager. Although individual personalities or attitudes may cause occasional problems, the team itself is much more important than any one individual player.

WHY TEAMS WORK

No matter the sport, a team's goal is clear: to score as much as possible to win. But in the workplace teamwork can be more complicated. People may want to play by their own rules. They might want to follow their own goals. And although ideally there shouldn't be opposition among employees, some people may have an opponent in a boss, manager, or even the person working next to them.

In a game, having a rival to play against is a great motivator. It gives a team a common focus, a shared "enemy" to combine forces against to win. At a job, this competitive instinct can be good if it's productive. Rivalry can get your adrenaline and ideas flowing. But when the enemy is someone within your company, the results are not productive. Instead of working together toward a common goal, colleagues can end

LET'S GO TEAM

Teams at work can be a lot like sports teams. You are all working toward common goals. Randy Rager, head coach at Rochester Community and Technical College, told Matt Krumrie for USA Wrestling that the best thing a teammate can do is be supportive. He suggested one give support by:

- "Being inclusive of others."
- "Being leaders" at work, at home, and in the community.
- "Being honest and holding others accountable while also accepting feedback from others."
- "Working hard and leading by example."
- "Having a positive attitude and willingness to teach others."
- "Having a positive and energetic outlook even during struggles and difficult times."

These attributes helped Rager's team become national champions twice. If you follow these suggestions, you'll be winning at work, too.

up gossiping, complaining, and working against one another. This turmoil can waste time and energy. You could be working instead of dealing with drama. It also creates a potentially stressful and unhappy work environment where trust may become an issue.

WORKING TOGETHER WORKS

Groups of people can work together in many different ways. There is no single model of a team. Instead, a team's organization will depend on many factors.

These can range from the kind of business and where it is located to the needs and wants of owners and customers.

Some teams consist of people who sit together in a common workspace. Throughout the day, they talk to one another about projects. They deal with problems that come up. In other cases, people on the same team might sit in separate spaces. They might meet up once a day, once a week, or even once a month. They do their own thing but get together every once in a while to discuss projects and trade ideas.

These days, many workplaces are remote. This means you might never meet your coworkers in person, but you can still forge relationships via text and chat.

Some people might never even meet in real life, instead working remotely via their laptops, from their home, the library, or another quiet place they enjoy. They might live in different cities, states, or even countries. These teams don't need to get together in person. They don't chat in a conference room or by the water cooler. Instead they keep in touch via cell phones, online chats, email, and conference calls. Despite these differences, every team shares values and objectives.

GETTING PUMPED

Being motivated is part of what makes a team work. Motivation occurs when people are kept interested and enthusiastic in meeting their own goals and common team goals. If your team members are gung ho about getting the job done, everything will run smoothly.

How are people motivated? There are several things you can do at work to stay enthusiastic.

- **Get involved.** When your boss, manager, or company involves you and your coworkers in the business's operations, people feel important. You, too, can involve your coworkers. Make them feel included, and let them know that you take their

Being a good team member means getting involved. Don't just focus on your tasks, offer to help others as well once your own work is done.

thoughts and contributions seriously. Ask how you can help complete tasks that will meet your team's goals.

- **Make clear goals.** Sometimes, people on a team work so hard that they lose sight of the end result. From time to time, it's important to sit down and reevaluate goals. You can also review each person's role.
- **Get out of the office.** Sometimes, it helps to get away from your work environment with your coworkers. Go somewhere where everyone can relax. It is often easier to examine how work relationships are functioning when you have an outside perspective.

It's important to discuss problems between team members. It's also essential to guide and encourage each other. High morale and confidence make a team successful.

WHEN TEAMS ARGUE: IT'S ALL ABOUT PERSPECTIVE

Sometimes team members don't get along. And while not every problem can be resolved, most can be improved. More importantly, by changing your attitude about a situation, you will feel better about your job and yourself. Others may also change the way they see you. Blaming others, making excuses, or getting angry or defensive doesn't improve a situation. If you concentrate on solutions instead of problems, obstacles can become opportunities. Soon, your team can get back on track.

Problems with coworkers? Sometimes considering their perspective, and where they are coming from, can help.

LEARNING FROM CUSTOMERS

If you work in the service industry—a restaurant or store, for example—don't let it get you down when customers complain. Instead, try to put your hurt or anger aside. Try to see past the complaint to any helpful, constructive criticism it might contain. This can help you provide even better service or do an even better job. Your efforts will not only prove to clients that you are listening to them. They will also show that you are a professional.

Lizzie was frustrated when her customer complained about how her groceries were bagged. She was going as fast as she could! But she took a moment to look at her customer, an older woman who had a cart with wheels to walk her groceries home. Lizzie realized that the bags needed to fit in the woman's cart, and be light enough for the woman to lift when she got home. She took a deep breath and fixed the bags for the woman. The woman smiled and thanked Lizzie many times. Lizzie's frustration was gone. She had solved a problem and gotten better at her job. She had helped out her team.

GETTING ALONG WITH COWORKERS

Remember that at work, you do not have to be best friends with everyone. But you should always try to be professional and polite. How well or poorly you get along with other people can have a major impact on your experience at work.

John doesn't like his boss because he's always on his case. One day, John's boss criticizes part of his work, but complimented his overall performance. Instead of basking in his boss's praise, John focused on his critical comments because they fed into his dislike for his boss. Meanwhile, John and his colleague Marie had a good relationship, where they always encouraged and supported each other. Because of the confidence and friendship they shared, John appreciated when Marie gave him a tip on how to improve his job. He was glad Marie told him the truth. He was able to listen without becoming defensive. Try keeping perspective when you are talking with a coworker, even one you have had trouble with in the past. Perspective can help make your team stronger.

By dealing with criticism, staying motivated, and working together as a team, your coworkers will value your contributions.

CHAPTER FOUR

STANDING UP FOR YOURSELF

D o you avoid confrontation? Do you worry that you're too nice at work? Does this make people take advantage of you? From time to time, everyone says or does things to please someone else. Then you might wonder, "Why didn't I say no?", "Why didn't I stand up for myself?", or "Why didn't I say what I really think?"

Having a job means sometimes you have to do things you might not be in the mood for. Don't forget that you are getting paid to do a task. You should also try to respect your manager or boss. Attempt to comply with his or her rules and wishes. But remember, you were probably hired thanks to your personality, skills, and experience. And no matter what kind of job you have, it is important that you be allowed to communicate your ideas and display your talents. The skill of expressing yourself in a clear, honest, and positive way is known as being assertive.

Everyone encounters conflict at work sometimes. It can be uncomfortable and awkward, but you can assert yourself and solve the issue.

STANDING STRONG

Some people confuse assertiveness with aggressiveness. Aggressiveness means being hostile toward someone else. When someone is being aggressive, he or she will use an argument that goes beyond the topic at hand. He or she may attack the other person's character. Assertiveness is different. Assertiveness means standing up for yourself. For what you believe is right. While you should consider other people's rights and feelings, you also want them to be aware of yours. Assertiveness means letting people know what kind of treatment is acceptable to you and what isn't. It also has to do with taking responsibility, with expressing yourself effectively. Being assertive means wanting respect for your contributions, efforts, and ideas. Assertiveness also includes being able to stand up for yourself, actively disagree, express positive or negative feelings, and make requests.

THE IMPORTANCE OF CONFIDENCE

Lack of assertiveness can cause problems. If you act as if everything is fine but you really resent a cranky boss or a bossy coworker, these pent-up feelings can eat away at you. You may want to express your feelings, but you may not have the confidence to do so. Your anger might reach a boiling point. You might keep these feelings to yourself, which can be confusing and depressing. Or you could erupt, maybe at the wrong place and time. You don't want to yell at someone, like a family member or friend, who has nothing to do with your work frustrations. What if you at last let loose in front of your boss or coworker? Having held in your feelings for so long, your reaction may seem out of proportion to what finally made you snap. Instead of an outburst when you can no longer hold it in, it is a better idea to confidently deal with the problem.

ASSERTING YOURSELF

Being assertive doesn't mean bulldozing over other people's feelings. There are many ways to be assertive. You can be heard, understood, and respected, without losing your temper. Sometimes you will even get your way. You cannot always be assertive and nice at the same time. But you never have to be nasty.

One common assertiveness technique is called the three-part assertion message. Use it to explain your needs and to try to get people to change their behavior.

1. Describe the offending behavior.
2. Address how it affects you.
3. Focus on how it makes you feel.

Cindy was repeatedly late for meetings. Lauren was getting fed up. Lauren said to Cindy, "When you are late for our meetings [the offending behavior], I waste time waiting for you. I could be spending that time on work [how it affects you]. This is frustrating for me [how it makes you feel], and I'd like us to work on solving the problem." This last part of the statement leads to finding a solution.

For some other assertiveness techniques, consider this scenario: Josh's boss asked him to write a report. When Josh gave her the document,

There are many different ways you can react to criticism. By owning your feelings and offering solutions you can navigate your way through difficult situations.

she had a very negative reaction. Josh felt terrible. He was at a loss. But there are ways to take charge of the situation.

Boss: This report is terrible!
Josh: You're right. It is.
Boss: What do you mean, "It is"? It's full of grammar mistakes.
Josh: You're right, my grammar is awful.
Boss: Well, this is a problem.
Josh: You're right. I'm really bad at reports.

Josh's boss wasn't prepared for him to agree with her. By surprising her, Josh took control.

Boss: You're useless! Once again, you've handed in a terrible report!
Josh: I don't like it when you attack me. I'd prefer if you let me know what

the specific problem is. Then we can work on improving things.

Josh let his boss know how he felt. Then he took charge of the situation by proposing that they work together to make it better.

Boss: This report is terrible!
Josh: What's the matter with it?
Boss: It's full of errors.
Josh: Would you like me to do it over?
Boss: Yes. Have it back to me in three hours.
Josh: I need to finish another project first. But I can have it back to you tomorrow morning.

This is a type of negotiation where Josh and his boss end up winning. They both expressed themselves and the report gets done.

Depending on the situation, you can choose what reaction is most appropriate and comfortable for you. For instance, you might be stressed out by the thought of getting angry and standing your ground. Or you might not want to react negatively to an unfair or unkind comment. Give yourself the choice of how you react to a situation. You don't have to simply take whatever unfair treatment a coworker or boss is dishing out.

EXERTING YOUR INFLUENCE

Influencing other people is similar to being assertive. Inspiring and serving as a guide to your coworkers is a form of influencing. Instead of complaining or wishing things were different, influential people figure out what needs doing. They then use their interpersonal skills—verbal communication, body language, assertiveness, experience, and understanding—to guide others and get things done.

People are naturally drawn to those who are positive, determined, and considerate. People who can express themselves well. At work, influential people are respected and admired. Their ideas carry weight. Win their support, and they will back your ideas and projects. Being influential can make your job a lot easier.

STAY CALM AND THINK OF OTHERS

Assertiveness isn't aggressiveness. And influencing people isn't forcing them to do things your way. Bullying or nagging others to do something or see your point of view doesn't work. In fact, it will likely cause them to lose respect for you. They might even dislike you.

Successful influencers always take others' feelings and views into consideration. To guide others, one must be flexible. You have to adapt your interpersonal skills to different contexts and types of people.

If you want to influence people at work, you have to figure out what your coworkers need and want. Think about requirements and wishes. How can you build bridges and win over allies? If people sense they have things in common—likes, dislikes, ideas, or goals—they're much more likely to be sympathetic to one another.

Nate wanted his boss to purchase a new design program for work. It was expensive, but it would make

BE LIKE MALALA

She is the youngest woman to ever receive a Nobel Prize, at age 17. She's a successful best-selling author. She founded an international nonprofit to fight for girls' education. And she's a student at Oxford University in England.

Malala Yousafzai was 15 years old when she was shot by the Taliban. Malala had spoken out about the importance of educating women, and the Taliban wanted to silence her. They did not succeed. Malala survived and has gone on to be a powerful voice for change.

Malala is an influence all around the world. People listen to her. One of the causes she cares deeply about is female refugees, or people who had to quickly leave their country because of unsafe conditions. Malala had to leave her home and live in England after being targeted by the Taliban.

"I know what it's like to leave your home and everything you know," she said in a statement via *Teen Vogue.* "I know the stories of so many people who have had to do the same. I hope that by sharing the stories of those I have met in the last few years I can help others understand what's happening and have compassion for the millions of people displaced by conflict."

Malala is using her voice and her understanding of a situation to communicate to others the importance of this cause. She is using her influence to help the world.

Malala Yousafzai, an activist for female education, uses her influence to change the world. She speaks to a crowd in London in 2014.

Nate's job a lot easier. Nate knew his boss didn't like to spend money. The budget was tight, and his boss already needed to hire another person. How could Nate build a bridge between what he wanted and his boss's concerns? Nate wrote up an analysis showing how much time he could save using the new program. He explained how he would use that time to take on extra responsibilities. This meant there was no need to hire a new person. Nate saved his boss money and got what he wanted. He influenced the outcome by thinking through everyone's concerns.

You might get frustrated when someone doesn't understand your point of view, but keep in mind that he or she might also be frustrated. Instead of trying harder to get people to see things your way, try changing tactics. You will likely get better results if you speak in encouraging tones, use plenty of eye contact, and invite people to state their opinions. Show respect. People will be more willing to meet you halfway if they feel that you appreciate their points of view. They may even agree to do something they wouldn't normally agree to because you made them feel important.

10 GREAT QUESTIONS

TO ASK A MANAGER

1. What do you most care about at work?
2. How do you find out what your staff cares about?
3. What motivates you?
4. How do you motivate your staff?
5. How do you deal with staff conflict?
6. What's the one thing you wish your staff knew about your job?
7. How do you want your staff to voice concerns? In an email? In person?
8. How do you want to hear about staff ideas? In an email? In person?
9. What do you love most about being a manager?
10. What's your best tip for being a great manager?

CHAPTER FIVE

HANDLING CONFLICT

No one really likes conflict. But it happens. It can be stressful and tense, especially when conflict happens at work. You still have to get your job done, but you're upset. Have hope! You can use interpersonal skills to resolve workplace conflicts.

MISUNDERSTANDINGS

Conflict occurs when people disagree and can't find a solution. It can be hard to find a solution if you aren't communicating. You can't agree if you can't understand each other. Misunderstandings can occur when people:

It's natural to have misunderstandings at work. But dealing with the argument calmly and rationally is important. Remember, you still have to work together.

- Have different opinions
- Have emotional reactions
- Don't understand each other

NO FAIR!

When miscommunication occurs, it's natural to blame the other person. You might wish the other person would change. Because then everything would be resolved. "If my boss would just stop being so demanding, this job would be better." Or, "If my coworker would stop being so bossy, we would get along fine."

As the "difficult" person continues to complicate your work life, you may be storing up accusations. You may feel resentful. You might make up ways the person should change. You might even think the person is being annoying on purpose. *They're out to get you!*

If you are so busy feeling slighted, you might be unable to look at the conflict objectively. When you're feeling wronged, you're probably not looking at your own flaws.

Take a step back and analyze the conflict. Try to look at the other person's point of view. Is there any way that that person could claim that you are being unreasonable or difficult? Chances are that—rightly or wrongly—someone out there (whether a parent, sibling, friend, or coworker) finds you "difficult" at times as well.

HOW NOT TO HANDLE CONFLICT

When confronted with a conflict, most people will often react by doing one of the following:

- Avoiding the conflict
- Trying not to make waves
- Storing up evidence
- Complaining or gossiping
- Getting into a big blowout

These actions will not help. They might make you feel better, but they won't solve anything. They might even make things worse. By placing all the blame on the other person, you are making that person responsible for how you feel. You're giving that person control over your relationship.

HOW TO HANDLE CONFLICT

When dealing with conflict, remember that you have a choice. You can become a victim. Or you can try to take charge. If you use your interpersonal skills, you can manage the other person instead of allowing that person to manage you.

No matter how annoying, unfair, or mean you think someone else is, you can't count on that person to change. What you can change is the relationship. You can do this by changing how you act. You can change what you say to this person. Although you may not always get what you want, you will be more in charge of what happens.

BARGAINING, NEGOTIATING, AND MORE

If two people or groups can't agree on how to resolve a disagreement, they have three options. They can walk away, get into a fight, or find a solution that works

Conflict can be resolved. By having an open mind while standing up for what you believe in, you can negotiate compromises that work for everyone.

for both sides. Dealing with conflict by communication is called negotiating.

Negotiation isn't about one person winning and the other losing. It's about both sides feeling as if they got something they wanted. Negotiations are successful when both sides leave better off than when they first began. This is called a win-win situation. If one side feels better off but the other doesn't (a win-lose situation), the negotiation hasn't really been successful. You may have "won" this time, but chances are the person or people you "defeated" won't want to negotiate with you ever again. They also won't trust you.

Negotiating can involve different skills and techniques. There is no one model. Instead, the approaches will depend upon the individuals and situations with which you are confronted. For instance, sometimes negotiating involves talking issues through. If everybody's individual interests are taken into consideration, then an acceptable agreement can be reached. At other times, successful negotiation involves give and take. All have to give up one or more things they want.

When negotiating, you need to be flexible. Flexibility means you are able to see what your opponents want. Instead of stubbornly sticking to your position and refusing to budge, consider giving up one wish in exchange for another that you have a better chance of obtaining. Flexibility also means that when necessary, you can fight hard for something. But when the battle isn't worth it, you gracefully let it go.

THE IMPORTANCE OF BOUNDARIES

Letting people know how their behavior affects you is called boundary setting. Boundaries are limits. If you don't set clear boundaries—or if you say nothing at all—you are in a way saying that the way others treat you is OK.

When you set boundaries, you are taking charge. You are defining your relationship by communicating what kind of treatment is OK with you and what isn't. Even if the other person's attitude doesn't change right away, over time he or she will learn you will not accept certain behavior. Then you can negotiate a different way of communicating.

ASKING FOR HELP

Sometimes you'll run into conflicts where no resolution or negotiation is possible. This may be due to a variety of factors. In some cases, a person's behavior toward you may even be harassment or discrimination.

CONFRONTATION 101

Those who harass generally expect you to be silent or to scream. If you are too scared to say something, the bully has won. If you lose your cool and shout, the bully will be thrilled at having provoked a reaction. A good way to deal with bullies is to calmly confront them. Do not play by their rules.

Anger with Anger

Them: Your report is horrible! How did you even get this job?

You: You're a jerk! What is your dumb problem?

Calmness over Anger

Bully: Your report is horrible! How did you even get this job?

You: Shouting at me is not productive. I'm disappointed that you can't sit down and discuss this calmly.

Expressing how you feel and allowing for discussion is a way to take away a bully's power.

STOP BULLYING

Bullying is never OK. If you are being harassed or experiencing other harmful behavior at work, tell a supervisor and a trusted adult in your life.

If you are being harassed, discriminated against, or bullied, you may feel isolated. Do not keep a problem this serious to yourself. Talk to someone, like a manager or human resources person. Workplaces have laws and rules that are designed to protect workers from discrimination and harassment. However, a lot of people find it difficult to make a formal complaint. Some people are afraid no one will believe them or that they'll lose their jobs. Bring any written communication you have that showcases the problem, like emails, texts, or online chats. Stay calm and state your case. You might want to make some bullet points or notes ahead of time to keep your mind clear. Present the problem in a calm, rational manner. Instead of finger-pointing, offer particular examples of how you were treated and the consequences.

- Nonobjective way: "Jane hates me. Anytime I say something, she attacks me. She's out to get me."
- Objective way: "I've been having difficulty with Jane. Yesterday, during a meeting, she criticized my work in front of everyone and wouldn't give me an opportunity to present my point of view. Unfortunately, these conflicts have come up at the last four meetings."

A manager or human resources professional will have the skills and authority to deal with the offending person's behavior. He or she will also be able to provide you with advice and support.

YOU ARE READY

If you are able to learn and put into practice these interpersonal skills, you will be well prepared for any workplace. The truth is that if you can't connect with the people you work with, it probably won't matter how hard you work or how many brilliant ideas you may have. Job experts have found that emotional intelligence—the capacity to manage your emotions well—is just as important to success in the workplace as a high IQ or lots of expertise.

Workplace relationships can be fulfilling and fun. By working hard and being a team player, you can handle anything that comes your way!

Good interpersonal skills will help ensure day-to-day happiness at your job. They also will contribute significantly to your overall success—not only in the career that you choose but also in the life you lead.

adrenaline A burst of energy.

assertive Confident and self-assured.

boundaries Limits, both physical and mental, to separate oneself from others.

camaraderie A friendly and good feeling amongst a community.

comply To agree with or behave according to rules, desires, or demands.

context The environment or situation in which an event takes place.

credibility The ability to inspire confidence, acceptance, or belief.

defensive Constantly protecting oneself against criticism, whether real or perceived.

discrimination Prejudiced treatment or action against someone.

harass To continually disturb, bother, harm, or torment someone.

inflection The pitch, level, and volume of a voice.

monotone One unvaried tone used in a series of words or sentences.

morale Mental or emotional condition—like enthusiasm, confidence, or loyalty. A common sense of purpose within a group.

motivated Encouraged, stimulated.

navigate To steer; to make one's way through something.

negotiate To attempt to come to an agreement through discussion and compromise.

objective Relating to a situation or facts without taking personal feelings or prejudices into account.

perspective An evaluation of a situation or facts from an objective point of view.

reevaluate Reconsider.
slighted Treated with indifference.
tone Style or manner of expression.
unambiguous Clear and precise.

Apprenticeship.gov
200 Constitution Avenue NW
Washington, DC 20210
Phone: (877) US-2JOBS
Website: http://www.apprenticeship.gov
The US Department of Labor's extensive website has information on career planning and various apprenticeships.

DO-IT (Disabilities, Opportunities, Internetworking, and Technology)
University of Washington
Box 355670
Seattle, WA 98195-5670
(888) 972-DOIT (3648) or (206) 685-DOIT (3648)
Email: doit@uw.edu
Website: http://www.washington.edu/doit
Facebook & Twitter: @doituw
This program works to help those with disabilities achieve academically and in their careers, thanks to technologies that increase productivity and independence.

Emily Post Institute, Inc.
444 South Union Street
Burlington, VT 05401
(802) 860-1814
Website: http://emilypost.com/advice-type/business
Email: info@emilypost.com
Facebook: @emilypostinstitute
Twitter: @EmilyPostInst

Created by Emily Post in 1946 and run today by
   third-generation family members, the Emily Post
   Institute is dedicated to teaching social and
   business skills as well as manners for every
   occasion.

Employment and Social Development Canada
140 Promenade du Portage
Phase IV
Gatineau, QC K1A 0J9
Canada
(800) 827-0271
Website: http://www.canada.ca/en/services/jobs.html
Email: NC-NOC-CNP-GD@hrsdc-rhdcc.gc.ca
Twitter: @Job_Emplois
The Canadian government offers information on
   employment, including career-planning resources
   and job listings.

TeenWorks
2820 N Meridian Street
Suite 1250
Indianapolis, IN 46208
(317) 916-7858
Website: https://teenworks.org/
Email: info@teenworks.org
This organization, founded in 1981, helps teens to find
   summer jobs. Scholarship opportunities are also
   available.

Toronto Public Library Teens: Job Search Help
789 Yonge Street
Toronto, ON
M4W 2G8 Canada
(416) 393-7131
Website: http://torontopubliclibrary.typepad.com/teens
   /jobs.html
Email: teens@torontopubliclibrary.ca
Facebook: @torontopubliclibrary
Twitter: @torontolibrary
Find resources for job searching in Canada, along with
   mentorship and job shadowing information.

Youth.gov
(877) 231-7843
Email: youthgov@air.org
Website: http://youth.gov/youth-topics/youth
   -employment
A US government resource with internship and job
   listings, info on careers and certifications, and
   videos and podcasts.

FOR FURTHER READING

Alexander, Kwame, and Thai Neave. *The Playbook: 52 Rules to Aim, Shoot, and Score in This Game Called Life*. Boston, MA: Houghton Mifflin Harcourt, 2017.

Bard, Jonathan. *Collaboration in Computer Science: Working Together*. New York, NY: PowerKids Press, 2019.

Braun, Eric. *Never Again: The Parkland Shooting and the Teen Activists Leading a Movement*. Minneapolis, MN: Lerner Publications, 2019.

Freedman, Jeri. *Step-by-step Guide to Becoming a Leader at School & on the Job*. New York, NY: Rosen Publishing, 2015.

George, Liz. *Conflict Resolution: When Friends Fight*. New York, NY: Children's Press, 2016.

Landau, Jennifer. *Teens Talk About Leadership and Activism*. New York, NY: Rosen Publishing Group, 2018.

McLaughlin, Jerry, and Katherine E. Krohn. *Dealing with Your Parents' Divorce*. New York, NY: Rosen Publishing, 2016.

Moyle, Eunice, Sabrina Moyle, Alex Bronstad, and Blake Bronstad. *Be the Change: The Future Is in Your Hands*. Lake Forest, CA : Walter Foster Jr./ Quarto, 2018.

Nagelhout, Ryan. *Your Legal Rights in the Workplace*. New York, NY: Rosen Publishing, 2016.

Rich, KaeLyn. *Girls Resist!: A Guide to Activism, Leadership, and Starting a Revolution*. Philadelphia, PA: Quirk Books, 2018.

BIBLIOGRAPHY

American Association for the Advancement of Science. "Strategies for In-Person Engagements: Nonverbal Communication." Retrieved April 10, 2019. https://www.aaas.org/resources/communication-toolkit/strategies-person-engagements-nonverbal-communication.

Chopra, Deepak. "Deepak Chopra: How to Deal With Co-Workers You Can't Stand." Oprah.com, Accessed April 9, 2019. http://www.oprah.com/spirit/how-to-deal-with-bad-co-workers-ask-deepak.

Equipped for the Future Center for Training and Technical Assistance. "Teaching/Learning Toolkit." Retrieved May 2007. http://eff.cls.utk.edu/toolkit/standards_wheel.htm.

JobBank USA. "Ability to Delegate: Interview Questions." Retrieved May 2007. http://www.jobbankusa.com/interview_questions_answers/free_samples_examples/ability_to_delegate.html.

Krumrie, Matt. "How to be a Good Teammate." *USA Wrestling*, September 14, 2018. https://www.teamusa.org/USA-Wrestling/Features/2018/September/14/How-to-be-a-Good-Teammate.

Mehrabian, Albert. *Nonverbal Communication*. New Brunswick: Aldine Transaction, 1972.

Modestino, Alicia Sasser. "Why More Cities Should Offer Summer Jobs for Teens." *Harvard Business Review,* August 23, 2018. https://hbr.org/2018/08/why-more-cities-should-offer-summer-jobs-for-teens.

Okuszka, Jimmy. "15 Easy Ways To Make Friends In Your First Week On The Job." *Fast Company,* December 20, 2017. https://www.fastcompany

.com/40509736/15-easy-ways-to-make-friends-in
-your-first-week-on-the-job.

Park, Andrea. "Malala Yousafzai Is Writing a
Book About Her and Other Women's Refugee
Experiences." Teen Vogue, March 12, 2018. https://
www.teenvogue.com/story/malala-yousafzai
-announces-new-book-we-are-displaced.

Shipley, David, and Will Schwalbe. *Send: The Essential
Guide to Email for Office and Home.* New York, NY:
Alfred A. Knopf, 2007.

Shropshire, Corilyn. "Americans prefer texting to
talking, report says." *Chicago Tribune*, March 26,
2015. https://www.chicagotribune.com/business/ct
-americans-texting-00327-biz-20150326-story.html.

Thompson, Jeff, PhD. "Is Nonverbal Communication a
Numbers Game?" *Psychology Today*, September
30, 2011. https://www.psychologytoday.com/us/blog
/beyond-words/201109/is-nonverbal-communication
-numbers-game.

Van Wagner, Kendra. "Types of Nonverbal
Communication." About.com: Psychology. Retrieved
June 2007. http://psychology.about.com/od
/nonverbalcommunication/a/nonverbaltypes.htm.

INDEX

ABOUT THE AUTHORS

Elissa Thompson is a journalist who has been published in *USA Weekend*, the *Baltimore Sun*, and *In Touch Weekly*, among others. She received her master's in journalism from the University of Maryland. She has written and edited several other books for Rosen Publishing.

Michael A. Sommers is a writer and photographer. His numerous books for Rosen include various career-related titles.

PHOTO CREDITS